Ivan Nikitin

Ivan Vishniakov

Fiodor Rokotov

Dmitry Levitsky

Vladimir Borovikovsky

Orest Kiprensky

Alexei Venetsianov

Vasily Tropinin

Karl Briullov

Nikolai Gay

Vasily Perov

Ilya Repin

Ivan Kramskoi

Philip Maliavin

Mikhail Vrubel

Valentin Serov

Léon Bakst

Mikhail Nesterov

Konstantin Somov

Konstantin Korovin

Zinaida Serebriakova

Kuzma Petrov-Vodkin

Boris Grigoryev

Alexander Golovin

Boris Kustodiev

Ilya Mashkov

Piotr Konchalovsky

Aristarkh Lentulov

Natan Altman

Nicolai Fechin

Robert Falk

Marc Chagall

RUSSIAN *Painting*
Portraiture

AURORA ART PUBLISHERS · LENINGRAD

It was from delight in the perfection of man and the beauty of the surrounding world and the desire to capture it on canvas that portraiture was born.

The solidity and clarity of Rembrandt's brushwork, the delicacy and refinement of Gainsborough, Velázquez' attention to still-life detail, the virtuosity of Goya, David and Ingres, the Impressionists' passion for sunlight and air, the esoteric geometrism of Picasso and the cryptographic idiom of Modigliani all served to recreate on canvas the ever-changing face of Europe, viewed, as it were, in general terms, with social characteristics often distinctly prevailing over psychological insight. These artists' portrayals illustrate the development of society in Europe.

Not so the Russian portrait. Here we have before us a gallery of individuals. Each artist focused his attention on features which most fully expressed the ideal of the time. It was precisely this quest for the ideal as embodied in the personality of an innovator or reformer that marked the works of the Russian school of portrait painting, from Ivan Nikitin's *Peter the Great* to later nineteenth- and early twentieth-century portraits depicting cultural figures who were the pride of their country.

Compiled and introduced by *Galina Ivashevskaya*
Translated from the Russian by *Inna Sorokina*
Designed by *Piotr Kanaikin*

p$\dfrac{4903020000-936}{023(01)-91}$ 53-90

ISBN 5-7300-0224-6

In Russia, the beginnings of portraiture go back to icon painting. How-

ever highly generalized, however closely they adhered to the strict canons which governed the painting of icons, images of Russian saints such as Princes Boris and Gleb, Sergius of Radonezh, or Metropolitans Alexius and Peter were always personal likenesses. Even at this stage, signs of a departure from tradition are to be observed. The "local" tier in the iconostases of Russian churches was generally composed of icons of local Russian saints, who had died and been canonized within living memory. Later on, icons came to include figures of the laity: tsars, who were considered to be divine; metropolitans (with scenes from their lives); and donors who presented gifts to the church. Further evolution led to the depiction of man without an aura of holiness, with all his human strengths and weaknesses and with his personal characteristics rendered to make him recognizable. The portrait gradually abandoned conventions; it grew away from two-dimensional painting, the figures acquired flesh and blood, and it developed into a new, separate genre, an art in its own right.

St Nicholas. 13th century
The Russian Museum, Leningrad

A new interest in secular subjects reflecting everyday life, which was growing stronger at every level of society, called for artistic response. In folk art, it produced colourful popular broadsheets (known as *lubok* prints) and provided themes for painted decorations on birch-bark boxes, wooden chests, caskets and other household objects. The painter Simon Ushakov remarked of his European colleagues that they "depict various things and events in pictures that are as real as life itself". In seventeenth-century Russia, true-to-life representation of man met with powerful opposition for both ideological and artistic reasons.

To Archpriest Habakkuk, one of the leaders of the Old Believers, lifelike figures meant everything that was low and mean: "Look at the holy icons," he grieved, "and see men who found favour in the eyes of God, the way good isographers paint them, with their faces, and arms, and legs... emaciated from fasts and labours... And now ye have changed their looks and paint them like yourselves, fat-bellied, fat-faced, with the arms and legs as thick as the stump of a tree... And all this is so painted from being flesh-minded, for ye heretics love flesh and turn away from things sublime... Woe, woe is ye, wretches! Ay, Rus, why dost thou crave for foreign manners and customs!"

The abstract Old Russian scheme of plastic expression did not disappear

all at once. It was openly preserved in the Old Believers painting and persisted in a half-overt, half-hidden form in the *parsuna* style. A link between old and new, a transitional style belonging to the past and the future at the same time, the *parsuna* style inherited from Old Russian painting its colour symbolism, its accentuated outline, linear treatment and traditional rhythm.

The earliest painted portraits (*parsunas*) show the subject half-length, looking straight at the viewer from the centre of the composition, and usually set in a shallow space. However great the changes demanded by current style or fashion, these dominant features are always retained.

Since the subject of portraiture is man, ideological content is of greater importance here than in any other branch of painting. This is one of the reasons why in Russian art, with its inherent sensitivity to social problems, and its ideal of justice, the portrait has always held a place of honour. This is especially true of the periods in Russian history when interest in human personality and the need for self-knowledge rose to a particularly high level.

In Russia, portrait painting grew to become an independent branch of art in the early part of the eighteenth century. The reforms of Peter the Great, which prepared the rise of a new culture, provided the impetus for the development of portraiture. Unlike the Old Russian culture dominated by religious tradition, this new culture was permeated with a secular spirit and displayed high susceptibility to external influences. The period was characterized by a growth of national consciousness and rapid advances in every area of life. The individual, regarded in the context of his life and his usefulness to society, became the central figure in painting: he was one of the "Tsar's own labourers", assisting the sovereign in the building of a new Russia. Thus the scale of values which prevailed during the Petrine epoch made portraiture a leading genre. The time demanded its own ideal of man: life formed him and art created his image.

Enriched by forms and methods associated with the "European manner", Russian art underwent a profound transformation. Nevertheless, it did not lose its national identity. It adapted and moulded foreign influences until, much changed, they eventually became an integral part of the Russian artistic idiom. This learning from foreign models was based on the selective principle of cultural assimilation. The traditional formula of Western European portrait — the Rococo composition with the figure seen in three-quarter view against a dark background — was filled with a new, national content, presenting to the world the image of the Petrine epoch.

The earliest secular Russian portraits were executed by artists who remained anonymous, like generations of icon painters before them. These were the likenesses of members of the All-Joking, All-Drunken Synod of Fools and Jesters, a "jolly company" formed by some of Peter's intimates for his amusement. Artistically, these works are far from being perfect. True, in some of the faces an attempt is made at realistic representation, as in the portraits of Andrei the Madcap (Apraxin) painted in the 1690s or of Yakov Turgenev produced not later than 1695, but the figure and costume are still treated in a schematic manner.

The *parsuna* style of early portraits had a lasting influence on Russian portraiture and even foreign artists working in Russia succumbed to it. In works of provincial schools this influence was felt as late as the early nineteenth century.

During the Petrine epoch, it was common practice to despatch Russian paint-

IVAN VISHNIAKOV. 1699—1761

Stepanida Yakovleva. *Ca* 1756
The Hermitage, Leningrad

ers to study abroad to improve their skill at the expense of the state. In 1716, when he sent Ivan Nikitin on such a tour, Peter instructed his wife, Catherine I, who made a trip to Europe at that time, to beg of King Augustus II, as a favour, that he order "from the painter Ivan a portrait of himself, and likewise of other persons... that it may be known that we also have good masters in our country".

The work of Ivan Nikitin occupies a special place in Russian eighteenth-century art. He was the first Russian painter to rise to the standard of his European contemporaries. Animated by a patriotic spirit, Nikitin's work embodied the public ideal of the Petrine epoch — working for the common good and common welfare, by which was meant first and foremost the interests of the state. The master's best portraits show a profound understanding of human psychology and a highly personal aesthetic outlook. The gallery of Nikitin's characters opens with Peter the Great (early 1720s) representing the purposeful, strong-willed Peter as Reformer. Although the use of chiaroscuro here is still conventional, the characterization itself is keen and truthful. The circular shape the artist chose for this portrait accentuates the energetic features of the Tsar to the best advantage.

Another portrait, depicting the Hetman of the Ukraine, painted in the 1720s, is a landmark in the history of Russian painting. Simple in composition and laconic in colouring, it is wonderfully rich in psychological content. We see before us a man of his time, active, stern and straightforward, one who rose to his position as a Tsar's associate not because of noble birth but through services rendered to the country. This is an early example of the informal, intimate portrait, even though it is executed within the limits of the dominant Baroque style.

In the work of the early Russian portraitists, interest in man and his environment found expression in a painting's scale and compositional structure. Prime importance was given to the model's high social status. This approach determined the evolution of the portrait for decades to come.

The art of Ivan Vishniakov was a peculiar blend of the Western European tradition and features inherited from the *parsuna* style. Most of the painter's long life was spent at his desk in the Office of Works. It wat but seldom that he could afford time to "paint persons from life". His pictures of Sarah-Eleanor and William Fermore (*ca* 1750) reflect the influence of the refined and fanciful Rococo art, alongsidē with such principles of the *parsuna* style as the static, flattened representation and the extremely detailed rendering of costume.

The *Unknown Woman in Russian Costume* (1784) by Ivan Argunov is probably the very first picture of a Russian peasant woman. The model's ·features are static, and the artist seems to have concentrated on her costume and headdress, depicted with scrupulous accuracy.

Towards the middle of the eighteenth century the social basis of Russian

art was considerably broadened. The foundation of the St Petersburg Academy of Arts gave a strong impulse to this process: the admittance of dozens of young people from the lower middle class, artisans and soldiers was an important factor in the democratization of art. Teaching at the Academy was based on the doctrine of a return to antiquity. Classicism was the leading style, and history painting, including mythological and biblical subjects, the leading genre. Russian neo-Classicism was characterized by deference to the classical tradition, belief in the power of reason and the ideal of harmony and balance. Portraiture was classed with the minor genres like landscape and still life, but it was nevertheless precisely in portrait painting that the greatest successes were achieved during the period.

Fiodor Rokotov, one of the foremost portrait painters of the eighteenth century, occupies a place of exceptional importance in the history of Russian art, although much of his life story is hidden in obscurity. His work stands apart from that of his contemporaries and shows a certain tendency towards reticence: Rokotov left no self-portraits, and most of his later works depict anonymous men and women. The faces in his portraits, lit, as it were, by an inner radiance, seem to emerge from some mysterious space filled with darkness. The general mood is one of tension and disquiet. This effect is created by the use of local colours and the dramatic contrasts of red and pale blue, which may be exemplified by the portrait of Grand Prince Paul (the future Tsar Paul I) at the age of seven. But the main thing about Rokotov's portrayals is the expression in the sitters' eyes: meditative, aloof, devoid of all worldly vanity. He records the rise of a new type of men in contemporary Russia: men with a sense of honour and dignity, whose grandsons would take their stand in Senate Square on 14 December 1825.[1] Ivan Bariatinsky, depicted in a portrait of the early 1780s, was a representative of this new generation.

Rokotov was the first Russian painter to attempt an insight into a woman's soul. Unshed tears fill the beautiful eyes of Mme Struiskaya in her portrait of 1772. The features of Countess Ekaterina Orlova (1779), a dazzling society beauty and a maid-of-honour to Catherine II, are overshadowed by deep sadness, as if the artist had a premonition of her close death. The tragedy of the Russian woman, intelligent, cultivated and refined, yet debarred from every path to creative development, wounded Rokotov's heart, and the viewer cannot help but share his attitude.

VLADIMIR BOROVIKOVSKY.
1757—1825

Countess Anna Bezborodko
and Her Daughters. 1803
The Russian Museum, Leningrad

[1] See footnote 2 on p. 11.

The work of Fiodor Rokotov, as well as that of Andrei Rublev long before him, is an example of great heights that Russian art has reached. Nevertheless both painters were forgotten and rediscovered only in the early twentieth century, when the striving towards the higher ideals gained a new impetus. The shining beauty of Rublev's *Old Testament Trinity* and Rokotov's unsurpassed portraits was returned to mankind.

A superb mastery of painting techniques and great artistic fertility distinguished Rokotov's contemporary Dmitry Levitsky. From his very first steps in art, it was clear that here was a painter of marvellous talent, with a remarkably keen eye for the material world. Levitsky enjoyed a well-deserved and lasting fame. Unlike Rokotov, who explored spiritual problems, Levitsky was drawn rather towards the external aspect of life. He was amazingly versatile and varied his style from the official to the intimate with the greatest ease, his subjects ranging from the Empress to a parish priest. This enabled him to create a sort of pictorial cross-section of contemporary society. In his programmatic canvas, *Catherine II as Legislator in the Temple of the Goddess of Justice* (1783), Levitsky showed the ageing Empress almost without flattery, only slightly softening her hard features and moderating the heaviness of her stout figure.

His famous series painted between 1773 and 1776, depicting the final-year pupils of the Smolny Institute for Young Ladies, is Levitsky's most important work. It consists of seven full-length portraits of the Misses Nelidova, Khrushchova and Khovanskaya, Rzhevskaya and Davydova, Levshina, Alymova, Borshchova, and Molchanova. The charm of youth, the joy of life, and an atmosphere of perpetual holiday pervade these canvases. Some of the girls' faces have a naive, others a playful expression, but each of them looks forward to a cloudless future, unmarred by grief or care. The ceremonial character of the works is accentuated by a peculiar compositional balance sustained throughout the series, its harmonious rhythms and shimmering, silvery colouring. The artist's painterly skill in rendering the texture of fabrics gives an almost tangible quality to the crisp silks of the girls' gala dresses.

The art of Vladimir Borovikovsky was of a transitional nature. His paintings reveal the beginnings of tendencies which were to reach maturity in the nineteenth century. Borovikovsky's aim for constant self-perfection, his interest in mysticism and his sentimentalist tastes in art are all reflected in his work. He created a gallery of idealized portraits depicting persons of noble birth as humane and cultivated members of a "kind-hearted society". For all that, there was no flattery or hypocrisy about him; the master simply painted not what he actually saw before him but what he thought essential for the preservation of the existing order of things. An elegiac, meditative mood tinges Borovikovsky's portraits of Paul I (1800), of Kurakin (1801—2), of Paul's daughters, Grand Princesses Alexandra and Elena (1796), of Lopukhina (1797) and Gagarina (1801). The colour scheme of a pale, greenish yellow and the transparent haze harmoniz with the sheen of silks and the glittering of precious stones. The airiness of gossamer veils is echoed by the airy lightness of verdure, which forms the usual background for Borovikovsky's graceful and refined figures. The painter shared the ideas of the Enlightenment on the exceptional, if not altogether decisive, importance of art as a means of promoting moral progress and social improvement.

The Romantic trend found in Russia particularly fertile soil for its growth

and development. Its aesthetic principles, based on the juxtaposition of the spiritual and the materialistic, and its belief in the absolute value of genius (according to Kant, genius does not obey the rules but creates them) proved to be singularly close to the ideas of many Russian artists.

OREST KIPRENSKY. 1782—1836

Ekaterina Avdulina. 1822 (?)
The Russian Museum, Leningrad

Alexander Radishchev (1749—1802), the first
Russian revolutionary thinker, writer and phi-
losopher, came of a noble family. In his book
Journey from St Petersburg to Moscow (1790)
he advocated revolutionary methods for the over-
throw of the monarchy and serfdom in Russia.

On 14 December 1825, an uprising aimed at the
abolition of the monarchy and the establishment
of a constitutional republic, took place in St Petersburg. Its initiators, later known as the Decembrists — Pavel Pestel, Kondraty Ryleyev,
Wilhelm Küchelbecker and others — expressed
in their works high ideals of civic duty and called
for active struggle for the realization of man's
right to freedom and for the rational organization
of society.

The Imperial Academy of Arts elaborated a
system of artistic education which was based on
classical traditions petrified into a body of strictly
enforced rules and "eternal" canons. The corner
stones of the system were in the following of an
absolute ideal of beauty, common to all times and
all nations; obligatory idealization of nature; and
a repertory of subjects far removed from real
life.

Orest Kiprensky never thought of himself as a portraitist. His chosen
field was history painting. Yet it was in his portraits, where he gave his sitters
a romantic treatment as "exceptional personalities in exceptional circumstances",
that his sense of history most fully asserted itself. His best work shows the
influence of the progressive views of Radishchev [1] and the Decembrists.[2]
This is clearly felt in his portraits of Evgraf Davydov and Princess Rostopchina
(both painted in 1809), and in the magnificent series of pencil portraits (1809—
15), works in which Kiprensky's talent is seen at its peak. Evgraf Davydov is
presented as typical of a whole generation of Russian men. Once a brilliant young
officer, a bon vivant and ladies' man, he became one of the heroes of the war
with Napoleon in 1812. During the reign of Nicholas I he retired and settled
on a distant estate to spend the rest of his life among his family and household, as was the lot of many war heroes.

The rich and sonorous colouring of Kiprensky's canvases seems to reflect
the energy and drive of the time. His later work includes beautiful romanti-
cized portraits of the poet Pushkin (1827) and the writers D. Philosophov
(1826) and Nikolai Gnedich (1828).

Russia owed the flowering of its art in the earlier half of the nineteenth
century to the appearance of a whole constellation of men richly endowed
with talent and possessing true spiritual greatness. The sway of official aca-
demicism[3] came to an end. The breakthrough was made by Briullov's large-
scale composition The Last Day of Pompeii (1833) together with Ivanov's
The Appearance of Christ to the People (1868), both of them dazzling flashes
of genius far exceeding the limits of the religious and historic genres, and by the
works of the Venetsianov school.

Alexei Venetsianov is remembered in Russian art history as the father
of Russian genre painting and the founder of a workshop where he taught
young peasant artists. A man of great humanity and moral courage, he broadened the sphere of artistic representation to incorporate the life of the peasants,
whom he depicted with sympathy and understanding. Venetsianov's portraits
and genre scenes show idealized peasant characters. He painted children con-
templating butterflies and girls gathering meadow flowers; his peasants lead a
simple and dignified life. Most of the master's canvases are conspicuous for their
solemn rhythm and clear colours. It is first and foremost in his use of red that
Venetsianov's exquisite sense of colour finds expression. Red has ever been the
touchstone of artistic taste: a study of icon painting or Renaissance pictures
will tell you that. Red, in combination with white and gold, forms the basis of
Venetsianov's individual style as a colourist. He does not draw a line between
the different branches of painting: his portraits contain genre elements, and his
genre scenes include portrayals. The current of Sentimentalism, which pro-
claimed the superiority of feeling over reason (ratio), made the common
man a subject of art, revealing the wealth of his spiritual world and his fine
gift of sympathy and compassion. Venetsianov's canvases show us idyllic scenes
set in natural surroundings, tinged with a mood of melancholy reflexion and
with intimate overtones. All social problems are passed over, the hardships
and poverty of peasant life kept out of sight.

The art of Vasily Tropinin comes rather close to Venetsianov's genre
painting, although his characters are chosen not from among the peasantry but
from among petty townsfolk and the lower middle class. As a portraitist, Tropinin is a descendant of Borovikovsky: his models are invested with a similar
lyrical calm and meditative mood. His portraits of Bulakov (1823), Vasily
Yakovlev (late 1830s), Konstantin Ravich (1825) and Alexander Pushkin
(1827) are painted with the greatest care and concentration. The artist studies his sitters' faces with a penetrating eye, striving to fathom the soul of the man
of the epoch.

In his brilliant formal portraits, Karl Briullov carried the tradition of Levitsky to the limits of perfection, and the academic trend reached its highest point. A favourite of fortune, crowned with fame, and virtually worshipped by his contemporaries, Briullov was a virtuoso of the brush, one of the most gifted of Russian artists. He succeeded in combining realistic representation with romantic feeling: this was a new word in the art of portait painting. In such of his portraits as *Countess Yulia Samoilova and Her Adopted Daughter Amazilia Pacini Leaving the Ball*, or *The Rider*, or *Grand Princess Elena Pavlovna and Her Daughter*, the models are divested of their customary position of prime importance, yielding pride of place to purely artistic aspects — compositional balance and harmony, colouring and rhythm. In the *Rider*, for instance, the artist's interest is divided between the lady, her horse, the little girl and natural scenery: each of the motifs has an equal share of his attention. This may be due to the fact that here the figures are regarded as mere staffage. In other works, where greater importance is attached to the models, as in the *Self-portrait* (1848) or the pictures of Nestor Kukolnik or Michelangelo Lanci, Briullov followed the classical European tradition, avoiding any devices which might deflect the spectator's eye from the subject.

A more democratic trend was developing alongside this grand-style paint-

NIKOLAI GAY. 1831—1894

The Writer Alexander Herzen. 1867
The Tretyakov Gallery, Moscow

ing. Interest in scenes of everyday life was much increased by the work of Pavel Fedotov. It was largely owing to his genius that genre painting gained a firm foothold in Russian art, providing a starting point for the realistic trend, the main current of future Russian painting. Fedotov took his subjects from life, and the tone of each work was a response to reality. His canvases, now tinged with irony, now bitterly sorrowful or even tragically despondent, all share one feature in common: love and compassion for suffering mankind.

Fedotov's work in portrait painting may be illustrated by his pictures of Nadezhda Zhdanovich (1849) and the Zherbin children (*ca* 1851), showing the unmistakable influence of watercolour and miniature portraits. Modest in size and unassuming in their artistic aims, they breathe sincerity and warmth. His portraits of military men was the earliest attempt at a critical approach to the subject which was to have a great future in Russian art. Depicting the everyday man, Fedotov introduced a new note into the art of portraiture.

The year 1863 marked a turning point in the history of Russian painting. Fourteen students left the Academy of Arts on the eve of graduation, refusing to paint their final-year programmatic pictures as a protest against the academic routine. This event was followed by the formation of the St Petersburg Painters' Association in 1864, and in 1870 of the Society for Travelling Art Exhibitions whose members were popularly known as the Itinerants. This was the beginning of a new stage in the evolution of Russian art: its democratic, prerevolutionary stage.

The Itinerants enjoyed unprecedented success. They numbered a whole galaxy of brilliant painters, from Vasily Perov and Nikolai Gay, Ivan Kramskoy (the leader of the group), and Vasily Polenov, Vasily Vereshchagin, Nikolai Yaroshenko, Nikolai Kasatkin, Ivan Shishkin and Alexei Savrasov to such figureheads of Russian realism as Ilya Repin and Vasily Surikov. Their work aroused tremendous response in Russian society; they exerted a formative influence on public life and became an integral part of national art history.

The new trend in painting, national in substance, popular in subject matter and strongly coloured with progressive social tendencies, gave the leading role to genre scenes. Yet the Itinerants produced portraits as well, some of them unquestionable gems. The demand for psychological analysis as the condition *sine qua non* in a portrait (perfectly justifiable, even though it would seem to leave aside much else that is important) is fully satisfied by the works of Perov, Kramskoi, Gay and Repin. They viewed each model as unique, striving to reveal the core of his or her personality, often at the expense of self-expression. The face was given priority over all other elements in the portrait.

No account of Russian painting would be complete if it failed to mention the Itinerants' portraits of the great Russian writers: *Leo Tolstoy* (1873) and *Nikolai Nekrasov* (1877) by Kramskoi; *Alexander Ostrovsky* (1871) and *Fiodor Dostoyevsky* (1872) by Perov; and Gay's *Alexander Herzen* (1867). The sitters were men of such moral integrity that no artistic devices were needed to produce a truthful portrayal: their faces spoke for themselves. To make the viewer feel the sitters' inner world and to give an insight into their tense spiritual life, was the ultimate aim of the portraitists, and they proved able to attain it, for they managed to rise to higher knowledge, to develop a keener vision, and to achieve closer sympathy with the great men they depicted than their predecessors in art.

Compositionally, their works were quite traditional, with the model centrally placed, accents of light and colour put on the face and hands, and a conventional plain background. But these portraits rise above tradition by the force of their intellectual and emotional message. More is achieved here than mere personal resemblance: an accomplithed portrayal, not just of contemporary types, but of men who were the honour and conscience of the age.

All this is still more true of the work of Ilya Repin, one of the greatest Russian painters. Portraiture was the corner stone of his art, its substance and foundation. Intent scrutiny of man and rare narrative skill lie at the root of Repin's work. These qualities explain the secret of his unsurpassed popularity. Both a portraitist and genre painter in one, not only did Repin record an infinite number of human types, but he also explored an infinite variety of human relationships, probing down into their hidden depths. In depicting actual people, he invariably rose to such heights of generalization that he may well be said to have left us a portrait of the entire society of his time. Repin felt an equally strong interest in each of his subjects, be they of noble birth or of the middle class, barge haulers or peasants. He always strove to be objective and free of prejudice.

Repin's portrayals of ordinary people are as perfect artistically and as carefully finished as any of his depictions of the great and famous. His pictorial and compositional devices are mostly simple. Some of his later works, such as the portraits of Varvara Ikskul von Gildenbandt (1889), Vladimir Spasovich (1891), Vera Repina (*Autumn Flowers*, 1892) or the portrait of Natalia Golovina (1896), record the artist's search for more pronounced compositional and light-and-air effects and his greater attention to the expressive potentialities of colour. Repin's preoccupation with the pictorial aspect is illustrated by his series of preparatory studies for a huge group portrait known as *Formal Session of the State Council* (1901—3). In some of the portrayals, colour is used sparingly, which tends to increase its expressive power. Thus, the character of Konstantin Pobedonostsev, the clever and cynical Procurator of the Holy Synod of the Russian Orthodox Church, is excellently outlined by a few skilful brushstrokes.

In contrast to Repin, whose interpretation of character developed from the specific to the general, Vasily Surikov proceeded from the general, i.e. the historical theme, to the individual man. He left but few true portraits, but his studies for many-figured compositions like *The Morning of the Execution of the Streltsy* (1881), *The Boyarina Morozova* (1887) or *Ermak's Conquest of Siberia* (1895) include folk types represented with wonderful force and deep understanding. These compositions are in fact monumental group portraits, resounding with the passions and storms of past epochs. An interest in the past

has always been a form of reaction against contemporary reality. Retro
spective art is often used to bring before the viewer the burning problems o
the day or to suggest a lack in modern life of events and characters as great a
those of old. Surikov's heroic historical tragedies were inspired by actuality: the
fight of the rising proletariat. They were also reminders of the not so distant past
of historic experience, a sort of visual aid to the knowledge of national history
Their purpose was to make people stop and look back and comprehend the
meaning of events of the past before venturing forward.

Important advances in landscape painting in the nineteenth century

VALENTIN SEROV. 1865—1911

The Actress Maria Ermolova. 1905
The Tretyakov Gallery, Moscow

and its increasing popularity exerted a great influence on other branches o
painting, including portraiture. This influence found a particularly strong expression in the Impressionist works of Konstantin Korovin and the "subjective
realism" of Valentin Serov.

Serov began his artistic career painting pure landscape, but soon went beyonc
its limits; throughout his life, however, he retained his eye for landscape
His *Girl with Peaches* (1887) and *Girl in Sunlight* (1888) demanded of the
artist the solution of both portraiture and landscape problems. In the firs
of these pictures, the influence of landscape painting is felt in the rendering o
the shimmering, sun-filled air and the spots of light on the walls, the tablecloth
the peaches and the figure of the girl, little Vera Mamontova. This influence
is as strong in the other canvas: the girl and the tree seem to merge together
and the entire painted surface is virtually alive with the play of light and colour

The work of his teacher, Repin, was a formative influence on the young Serov. This is felt in the laconic manner used in the portraits of Isaac Levitar
(1893), Nikolai Leskov (1894) and Nikolai Rimsky-Korsakov (1898)
Highly illustrative of Serov's approach is the portrait of young Felix Yusupov
(1903). Unlike Rokotov's Bariatinsky (who was of the same age when painted)
full of the potential energy of a generation with a future before it, Yusupov i
a man for whom everything is in the past: not his own, to be sure, but his ancestors'
The fate of a doomed class can be read in his face, effete, cold and bearing a
stamp of decline.

Serov's portraits seem to sum up the artistic searchings of the two preceding
centuries, forming the crowning phase of a long evolution. He was also the
last great master of the formal commissioned portrait of members of the
nobility. As a class, the nobility had exhausted their historic potential. In contras
to Repin's full-blooded and colourful depiction of his aristocratic patrons
Serov's characterization of Olga Orlova (1911), Zinaida Yusupova (1900—2)
Mikhail Morozov (1902) or the rich Henrietta and Vladimir Girshman (1907
and 1911) is expressed in language that is cold and cutting. The elaborate
composition and refined colour scheme of pearly greys serve but to emphasize
an empty mind behind a vacuous, mask-like face. The artist is frankly critica
of his models; his scrutiny is probing and often merciless.

In his search for an ideal, Serov turned to the world of the arts. Hi
portrait of Maria Ermolova (1905) is a majestic image of this great tragic
actress. The space in which her figure is placed is divided into several planes
a device used to lead the spectator's eye to the main focus of the picture, the
face of Ermolova.

In his portraits of painters, writers and actors, Serov showed them as a nobl
race of chosen men, far removed from the common run and forming, as it were
a Pantheon of votaries of art.

Serov's portraits of children occupy a special place in his work: *Mika Mo
rozov* (1901), *The Children. Sasha and Yura* (1899), *The Botkin Childre*
(1900). They are painted with the greatest sincerity and tenderness.

The early years of this century were marked by a play of conflicting and

PIOTR KONCHALOVSKY. 1876—1956

The Artist Georgy Yakulov. 1910
The Tretyakov Gallery, Moscow

often mutually exclusive forces, currents and ideas. The 1905 revolution, the outbreak of World War I and the ripening of the bourgeois-democratic and proletarian revolutions which were to break out in 1917 were the main factors which shaped the spiritual and cultural life of Russia during the period. Artistic activities were intensive and varied as never before.

At the end of the nineteenth century the World of Art group appeared (1890—1903, 1910—24), their aesthetic principles sharply opposed to those of the Itinerants. Its members were most active in book design and illustration, scenography, museum and exhibition work and the publication of art magazines. Some of them, of whom the most prominent were Alexandre Benois, Konstantin Somov, Léon Bakst, Alexander Golovin and Zinaida Serebriakova, also painted portraits. They brought to this art form the peculiar expressiveness and compositional refinement of the Russian version of Art Nouveau.

The 1905 Exhibition of the Russian Portrait: Its History and Present Condition, organized by Serge Diaghilev, was an event of great interest and importance. It demonstrated, for the first time, the wealth of traditions accumulated within the genre over the years and revealed its current aims and prospects. Characteristic of the period was a departure from simple realistic solutions and a tendency toward generalized, symbolic treatment, the creation of typified images. This found expression in a novel approach to problems of composition and colouring. The silhouette acquired structural significance, the contour was invested with special meaning, and the background grew into an independent element of characterization. The active role of the silhouette in early twentieth-century portraiture was enhanced by contrasts of light and dark, which led eventually to the ample use of pure black and white, colours which had hitherto fulfilled only secondary functions. Explorations of new ways to heighten the decorative expressiveness of colour contributed to the creation of works of strong emotional tension, particularly characteristic of the art of Valentin Serov, Kuzma Petrov-Vodkin, Boris Grigoryev and Nicolai Fechin.

The Apostle Paul. Early 15th century
The Tretyakov Gallery, Moscow

ANDREI RUBLEV. *Ca* 1360—1430

Portraiture

The art of portraiture in Russia went through a long process of evolution. At its inception the Russian school bore the imprint of centuries-long traditions of icon painting; enriched by contacts with Western European painting, it produced excellent portraitists as early as the eighteenth century. The representative, formal portrait of the Late Rococo and the local romantic trend of neo-Classicism, elaborated by Rokotov, Levitsky, and Borovikovsky, were brilliantly developed in the nineteenth century by Kiprensky, Briullov and artists of their circle. The democratic and realistic trend represented by Venetsianov, Tropinin and Fedotov reached its highest point in the realism of the Itinerants, best represented in the works of Kramskoi, Gay, Perov, Repin and Surikov.

The source of all art lies in the sphere of moral values. A striving for the ideal dominates the entire history of Russian portraiture. Some painters, such as Serov, sought to find it in men of genius; others, like Repin or Surikov, explored the depths of national character.

Yakov Turgenev. Before 1695
From the series portraying members
of the All-Joking, All-Drunken Synod
of Fools and Jesters
Oil on canvas. 105×97.5 cm
The Russian Museum, Leningrad

ЯКОВЪ : ТУРГЕНЕВЪ :

АЛЕКСѢІ : ВАСИЛКОВЪ

ANONYMOUS. First half
of the 18th century

Alexei Vasilkov. Early 18th century
From the series portraying members
of the All-Joking, All-Drunken Synod
of Fools and Jesters
Oil on canvas. 43×53 cm
The Russian Museum, Leningrad

АНДРЕ . БЕСАЩЕІ

Andrei the Madcap (Andrei Apraxin). 1690s
From the series portraying members
of the All-Joking, All-Drunken Synod
of Fools and Jesters
Oil on canvas. 93×88 cm
The Russian Museum, Leningrad

ANONYMOUS. 18th century

Ermak Timofeyevich, Conqueror of Siberia.
First third of the 18th century
Oil on canvas. 98×75 cm
The Russian Museum, Leningrad

ANONYMOUS. First half
of the 18th century

Afanasy Radishchev. 1730s —1740s
Oil on canvas. 90×69 cm
The Radishchev Art Museum, Saratov

ANDREI MATVEYEV. 1701/4—1739

**Self-portrait of the Artist
with His Wife Irina. 1729 (?)**
Oil on canvas. 75.5 × 90.5 cm
The Russian Museum, Leningra

IVAN NIKITIN. 1680s — after 1742

Peter the Great. Early 1720s
Oil on canvas. Diam. 55 cm
The Russian Museum, Leningrad

Hetman of the Ukraine. 1720s
Oil on canvas. 76 × 60 cm
The Russian Museum. Leningrad

IVAN NIKITIN. 1680s — after 1742

IVAN VISHNIAKOV. 1699—1761

Sarah-Eleanor Fermore. *Ca* **1750**
Oil on canvas. 138×114.5 cm
The Russian Museum, Leningrad

Vasily Daragan. 1745
Oil on canvas. 101 × 85 cm
Museum of Art and History, Chernigov

IVAN ARGUNOV. 1729—1802

Unknown Woman in Russian Costume. 1784
Oil on canvas. 67×53.6 cm
The Tretyakov Gallery, Moscow

FIODOR ROKOTOV. 1730s —1808

Alexandra Struiskaya. 1772
Oil on canvas. 59.8×47.5 cm
The Tretyakov Gallery, Moscow

FIODOR ROKOTOV. 1730s —1808

Grand Prince Paul as a Child. 1761
Oil on canvas. 58.5 × 47.5 cm
The Russian Museum, Leningrad

FIODOR ROKOTOV. 1730s —1808

Unknown Lady in a White Cap. 1790s
Oil on canvas. 73×57 cm
The Russian Museum, Leningrad

FIODOR ROKOTOV. 1730s —1808

Prince Ivan Bariatinsky
as a Youth. Early 1780s
Oil on canvas. 64.2×50.2 cm
The Tretyakov Gallery, Moscow

FIODOR ROKOTOV. 1730s —1808

Countess Ekaterina Orlova. 1779 (?)
Oil on canvas. 42.5×56 cm
The Tretyakov Gallery, Moscow

FIODOR ROKOTOV. 1730s —1808

Countess Elizaveta Santi. 1785
Oil on canvas. 72.5 × 56 cm
The Russian Museum, Leningrad

DMITRY LEVITSKY. 1735—1822

The Architect Alexander Kokorinov, Director and First
Rector of the Academy of Arts in St Petersburg. 1769
Oil on canvas. 134×102 cm
The Russian Museum, Leningrad

DMITRY LEVITSKY. 1735—1822

Catherine II as Legislator in the Temple
of the Goddess of Justice. 1783
Oil on canvas. 261×201 cm
The Russian Museum, Leningrad

DMITRY LEVITSKY. 1735—1822

Countess Praskovya Vorontsova
as a Child. Ca 1790
Oil on canvas. 62.5 × 49.5 cm
The Russian Museum. Leningrad

Ekaterina Nelidova. 1773
Oil on canvas. 164×106 cm
The Russian Museum, Leningrad

DMITRY LEVITSKY. 1735—1822
Leningrad

DMITRY LEVITSKY. 1735—1822

The Writer Nikolai Novikov. 1797
Oil on canvas. 59.7×47.6 cm
The Tretyakov Gallery, Moscow

DMITRY LEVITSKY. 1735—1822

Nikolai Lvov, Architect, Painter
and Poet. 1780s
Oil on canvas. 71×55.5 cm
The Russian Museum, Leningrad

VLADIMIR BOROVIKOVSKY. 1757—1825

Vice-Chancellor Prince
Alexander Kurakin. 1801—2
Oil on canvas. 259×175 cm   →
The Tretyakov Gallery, Moscow

VLADIMIR BOROVIKOVSKY. 1757—1825

Maria Lopukhina. 1797
Oil on canvas. 72×53.5 cm
The Tretyakov Gallery, Moscow

The Actor Yakov Shumsky. 1760
Oil on canvas. 66.5×52.5 cm
The Russian Museum, Leningrad

OREST KIPRENSKY. 1782—1836

Ekaterina Rostopchina. 1809
Oil on canvas. 77×61 cm
The Tretyakov Gallery, Moscow

OREST KIPRENSKY. 1782—1836

Alexander Pushkin. **1827**
Oil on canvas. 63×54 cm
The Tretyakov Gallery, Moscow

** OREST KIPRENSKY. 1782—1836**

Self-portrait. 1828
Oil on canvas. 48.5×42.3 cm
The Tretyakov Gallery, Moscow

OREST KIPRENSKY. 1782—1836

Evgraf Davydov, Colonel in the Life Guards. **1809**
Oil on canvas. 162×116 cm
← The Russian Museum, Leningrad

Peasant Woman with a Scythe
and Rake (Pelageya). Before 1825
Oil on panel. 22.5×17.5 cm
The Russian Museum, Leningrad

ALEXEI VENETSIANOV. 1780—1847

Zakharka. 1825
Oil on cardboard. 39.8×30.7 cm
The Tretyakov Gallery, Moscow

VASILY TROPININ. 1776—1857

Bulakov. 1823
Oil on canvas. 66×55 cm
The Tretyakov Gallery, Moscow

VASILY TROPININ. 1776—1857

The Lace-maker. 1823
Oil on canvas. 74.7×59.3 cm
The Tretyakov Gallery, Moscow

Natalia Obolenskaya. **1833**
Oil on canvas. 108.7×90 cm
The Art Museum, Odessa

KARL BRIULLOV. 1799—1852

Self-portrait. 1848
Oil on cardboard. 67×54 cm
The Russian Museum, Leningrad

Countess Julia Samoilova and Her Adopted
Daughter Amazilia Pacini Leaving
the Ball. Before 1842
Oil on canvas. 249×176 cm
The Russian Museum, Leningrad

KARL BRIULLOV. 1799—1852

The Shishmariov Sisters. 1839
Oil on canvas. 281×213 cm
The Russian Museum, Leningrad

KARL BRIULLOV. 1799—1852

Princess Elizaveta Saltykova. 1841
Oil on canvas. 200×142 cm
The Russian Museum, Leningrad

KARL BRIULLOV. 1799—1852

The Rider: Portrait of Giovanina
and Amazilia Pacini. 1832
Oil on canvas. 291.5×206 cm
The Tretyakov Gallery, Moscow

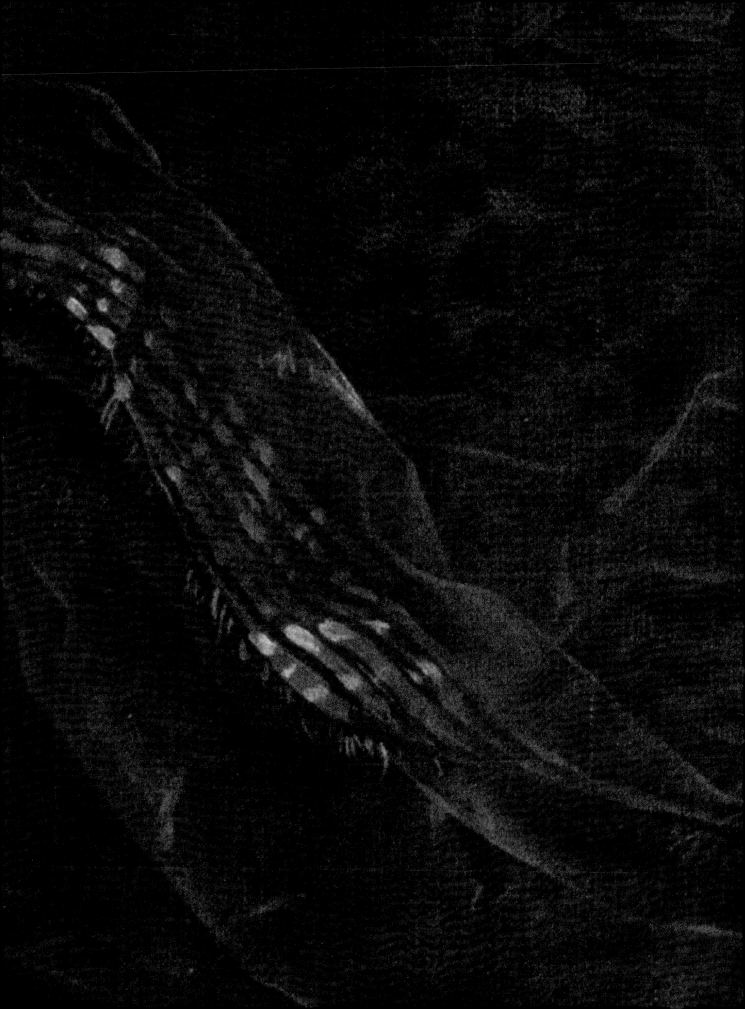

PAVEL FEDOTOV. 1815—1852

Nadezhda Zhdanovich at the Piano. 1849
Oil on canvas. 24.5×19.2 cm
The Russian Museum, Leningrad

ALEXANDER IVANOV. 1806—1858

Girl from Albano Standing in the Doorway
Oil on canvas. 43×31 cm
The Tretyakov Gallery, Moscow

KONSTANTIN MAKOVSKY. 1839—1915

Yulia Makovskaya, the Artist's Wife. 1881
Oil on canvas. 184×78 cm
The Russian Museum, Leningrad

NIKOLAI GAY. 1831—1894

Natalia Petrunkevich. 1892—93
Oil on canvas. 161.8×114.6 cm
The Tretyakov Gallery, Moscow

NIKOLAI GAY. 1831—1894

Maria Gabayeva. 1886
Oil on canvas. 60×49 cm
The Art Museum, Odessa

Self-portrait. 1892—93
Oil on canvas. 69.5×52.5 cm
Museum of Russian Art, Kiev

VASILY PEROV. 1834—1882

Self-portrait. 1870
Oil on canvas. 59.7 × 46 cm
The Tretyakov Gallery, Moscow

VASILY PEROV. 1834—1882

The Writer Fiodor Dostoyevsky. 1872
Oil on canvas. 99 × 80.5 cm →
The Tretyakov Gallery, Moscow

ILYA REPIN. 1844—1930

The Art Critic Vladimir Stasov. 1883
Oil on canvas. 74×60 cm
The Russian Museum, Leningrad

ILYA REPIN. 1844—1930

Self-portrait. 1878
Oil on canvas. 60.5×49.6 cm
The Russian Museum, Leningrad

ILYA REPIN. 1844—1930

The Composer Modest Mussorgsky. 1881
Oil on canvas. 69×57 cm
The Tretyakov Gallery, Moscow

ILYA REPIN. 1844—1930

**Autumn Flowers: Portrait of Vera Repina,
the Artist's Daughter. 1892**
Oil on canvas. 111×65 cm
The Tretyakov Gallery, Moscow

VASILY SURIKOV. 1848—1916

**Olga Surikova, the Artist's Daughter,
as a Girl. 1888**
Oil on canvas. 135×80 cm
The Tretyakov Gallery, Moscow

Mina Moiseyev. 1882
Oil on canvas. 57×45 cm
The Russian Museum, Leningrad

IVAN KRAMSKOI. 1837—1887

The Artist Ivan Shishkin. 1880
← Oil on canvas. 94.5×71.5 cm
The Russian Museum, Leningrad

IVAN KRAMSKOI. 1837—1887

Portrait of an Unknown Woman. 1883
Oil on canvas. 75.5×99 cm
The Tretyakov Gallery, Moscow

NIKOLAI YAROSHENKO. 1846—1898

Girl Student. 1880
Oil on canvas. 85×54 cm
Museum of Russian Art, Kiev

VICTOR BORISOV-MUSATOV. 1870—1905

Self-portrait with Elena, the Artist's
Sister. 1898
Oil on canvas. 143×177 cm
The Russian Museum, Leningrad

MIKHAIL VRUBEL. 1856—1910

The Opera Singer Nadezhda Zabela-Vrubel,
the Artist's Wife. 1898
Oil on canvas. 124×75.7 cm
The Tretyakov Gallery, Moscow

MIKHAIL VRUBEL. 1856—1910

Savva Mamontov, Moscow Businessman
and Patron of the Arts. 1897
Oil on canvas. 187×142.5 cm
The Tretyakov Gallery, Moscow

Mika Morozov: Portrait of Mikhail Morozov
as a Boy. 1901
Oil on canvas. 62.3×70.6 cm
The Tretyakov Gallery, Moscow

VALENTIN SEROV. 1865—1911

Girl with Peaches: Portrait
of Vera Mamontova. 1887
Oil on canvas. 91×85 cm
The Tretyakov Gallery, Moscow

Felix Yusupov, Count Sumarokov-Elstone. 190.
Oil on canvas. 89×71.5 cm
The Russian Museum, Leningrad

VALENTIN SEROV. 1865—1911

The Artist Isaac Levitan. 1893
Oil on canvas. 82×86 cm
The Tretyakov Gallery, Moscow

Princess Olga Orlova. 1911
Oil on canvas. 237.5 × 160 cm
The Russian Museum, Leningad

VALENTIN SEROV. 1865—1911
Leningad

VALENTIN SEROV. 1865—1911

The Dancer Ida Rubinstein. 1910
Charcoal and tempera on canvas. 147×233 cm
The Russian Museum, Leningrad

LÉON BAKST. 1866—1924

Serge Diaghilev and His Nurse. 1906
Oil on canvas. 161×116 cm
The Russian Museum, Leningrad

MIKHAIL NESTEROV. 1862—1924

The Philosophers: Portrait of Sergei Bulgakov
and Pavel Florensky. 1917
Oil on canvas. 123×125 cm
The Tretyakov Gallery, Moscow

KONSTANTIN SOMOV. 1869—1939

The Art Historian Andrei Somov,
the Artist's Father. 1897
Oil on canvas. 95 × 65 cm
The Russian Museum, Leningrad

Lady in Blue: Portrait of Elizave
Martynova. 1897—1900
Oil on canvas. 103×103 cm
The Tretyakov Gallery, Moscow

KONSTANTIN SOMOV. 1869—1939

The Actress Tatyana Liubatovich. 1880s
Oil on canvas. 160×84 cm
The Russian Museum, Leningrad

KONSTANTIN KOROVIN. 1861—1939

KONSTANTIN KOROVIN. 1861—1939

The Opera Singer Fiodor Chaliapin. 1905
Oil on canvas. 65×46.1 cm
The Tretyakov Gallery, Moscow

Breakfast: Portrait of the Artist's
Children. 1914
Oil on canvas. 88.5×107 cm
The Tretyakov Gallery, Moscow

ZINAIDA SEREBRIAKOVA. 1884—1967

ZINAIDA SEREBRIAKOVA. 1884—1967

Woman at Her Toilet: Self-portrait. 1909
Oil on canvas mounted on cardboard. 75×65 cm
The Tretyakov Gallery, Moscow

KUZMA PETROV-VODKIN. 1878—1939

Maria Petrova-Vodkina, the Artist's Wife. 1⁹
Oil on canvas. 80×65 cm
The Russian Museum, Leningrad

KUZMA PETROV-VODKIN. 1878—1939

Portrait of a Boy. 1913
Oil on canvas. 80×64 cm
The Art Gallery, Perm

BORIS GRIGORYEV. 1886—1939

The Photographer M. Scherling. Early 1910s
Oil on canvas. 99.3×80.5 cm
The N.F. Paleyeva collection, Leningrad

BORIS GRIGORYEV. 1886—1939

Mother: Portrait of Elizaveta Grigoryeva,
← the Artist's Wife, and His Son Kirill. 1915
Oil on canvas. 106×106.5 cm
The Russian Museum, Leningrad

The Producer Vsevolod Meyerhold. 1916
Oil on canvas. 247×168 cm
The Russian Museum, Leningrad

BORIS GRIGORYEV. 1886—1939

ALEXANDER GOLOVIN. 1863—1930

Fiodor Chaliapin as Boris Godunov
in Mussorgsky's Opera. 1912
Size paints, gouache, pastel, chalk, gold
and silver foil on canvas. 211.5×139.5 cm
The Russian Museum, Leningrad

BORIS KUSTODIEV. 1878—1927

The Artist Ivan Bilibin. 1901
Oil on canvas. 142×110 cm
The Russian Museum, Leningrad

BORIS KUSTODIEV. 1878—1927

Renée Notgaft. 1914
Oil on canvas. 110×82 cm
The Russian Museum, Leningrad

VICTOR VASNETSOV. 1848—1926

Mikhail Vasnetsov, the Artist's Son. 1892
Oil on canvas. 80×63 cm
The Art Museum of the Byelorussian SSR, Minsk

BORIS KUSTODIEV. 1878—1927

Yulia Kustodieva, the Artist's Wife. 1909
Tempera on cardboard. 96×71 cm
The Art Museum, Odessa

ILYA MASHKOV. 1881—1944

Lady with Pheasants: Portrait of F. Hesse. 1911
Oil on canvas. 177×133 cm
The Russian Museum, Leningrad

MARC CHAGALL. 1887—1985

Father (Father and Grandmother). 1914
Tempera on paper mounted on cardboard.
49.4×36.8 cm
The Russian Museum, Leningrad

Self-portrait (Le Grand Peintre). 1915
Oil and paper cutouts on cardboard mounted
on canvas. 142×104 cm
The Tretyakov Gallery, Moscow

ARISTARKH LENTULOV. 1882—1943

Self-portraits as Harlequin and Pierrot. 1914
Oil on canvas. 210×142 cm
The Russian Museum, Leningrad

VASILY SHUKHAYEV. 1887—1973
ALEXANDER YAKOVLEV. 1887—1939

VLADIMIR LEBEDEV. 1891—1967

Katka. 1918
Oil on canvas. 126×66 cm
The Russian Museum, Leningrad

KONSTANTIN ISTOMIN. 1887—1942

Portrait of a Woman. 1922
Oil on canvas. 73.5×69 cm
The Radishchev Art Museum, Saratov

ROBERT FALK. 1886—1958

Unknown Woman Wearing a Turban. 1910s
Oil on canvas. 118×84 cm
The Chudnovsky family collection, Leningrad

PIOTR KONCHALOVSKY. 1876—1956

Sophia Konchalovskaya, the Artist's Sister,
and Her Daughter Tatyana. 1916
Oil on canvas. 199×200 cm
The Russian Museum, Leningrad

NATALIA GONCHAROVA. 1881—1962

Self-portrait with Yellow Lilies. 1907
Oil on canvas. 77×58.2 cm
The Tretyakov Gallery, Moscow

Revealing the different aspects of human nature in members of every social group, Russian portraitists recreated in their works the many-faceted and contradictory character of a people at once talented and open-hearted, impetuous and contemplative, fired with a love of freedom and thirsting for justice. The images of a man ready to shoulder responsibility for the world's future and of a woman with a gift of deep feeling and great spiritual force have always been, and remain, central to the art of Russian portrait painting.

РУССКАЯ ПОРТРЕТНАЯ ЖИВОПИСЬ

Альбом (на английском языке)

Издательство «Аврора». Ленинград. 1991
Изд. № 1903. (17-00)
ЛПО «Типография имени Ивана Федорова»
Printed and bound in the USSR